the social agent

the new era of
social networking

Tony Giordano

ISBN: 1466317272
ISBN 13: 9781466317277

Library of Congress Control Number: 2011916272
CreateSpace, North Charleston, SC

table of contents

This book is dedicated to my two sons, Michael and Christopher, and my papa, who are three people that make me feel limitless. To everyone else in my life who inspired me to fulfill this passion of mine, thank you.

acknowledgments

The author has several people he would like to thank...

"I would like to start by thanking my Great-Uncle Mike for his overwhelming support and belief in me time and time again."

"Special thanks to Craig Duswalt for literally lighting the fire under me to finally start and finish my first book."

"Thank you to the following people for their contributions whether proof reading or being quoted in the book. Allana Baroni, Jay Rubenstein, David Marine, John Schumacher, Steve Gatena, Josh Patz and Lewis Howes"

"Special thanks to Eric Qualman author of 'Socialnomics', and Chris Anderson and Michael Wolff, authors of 'The Web is Dead'. These are individuals who inspired me to write my book based on their own writing accomplishments and teachings."

"Thank you to John Hildebrand Photography for the book cover, and www.CreateSpace.com for making the publishing, design and editing process so easy for me."

"Last but not least I would like to thank Starbucks Coffee for making such comfortable cafe's that I wrote the majority of my book in..."

introduction

First I want to say thank you for choosing to read my book. Being an author has been a goal of mine for years, and I finally just locked myself in my home to get it done. Well, I wrote a lot of it at the coffee shop, too. ☺ I think it had something to do with finally having the right topic to write about and a topic that would help real estate agents as well as business executives with their success. Now, although this book will go into many details about social media, trade secrets, and the correct strategies to execute, it does not replace the advantages of one-on-one training and/or having a consultant come in and teach you or your company. The book's main role is to show you the importance of social media and the *correct way to practice* it. This book will give you a very common-sense and easy approach to social networking. My vision is for you to read it with your smart phone (iPhone, Droid, etc.) and/or tablet (iPad, for example) close by. If you do not have either of those, a computer is fine. The reason is I want you to try things I say in this book while you are reading that particular chapter. Interaction while reading has always been rewarding for me, although I'm sure some will prefer to read and then skim through a second time while practicing. I have left a blank page at the end of each chapter for you to write down your own thoughts. You will have some and you won't want to forget them. You will also see in this book abbreviations and smiley faces; we all text and write abbreviated nowadays. Why not write a more modern book, then? ☺

To say I am from Southern California would be putting it lightly. I truly consider the overall So-Cal area home. In a nutshell, my family and I moved around a lot while I was growing up. I was born in Beverly Hills, California, and we moved to Ventura Beach, California, when I was about one. From there, I was all over So-Cal. When I look back on my years growing up, I wouldn't trade them for anything. I was never 'comfortable' and I am glad. I always needed to make new friends, meet new people, and, boy, was I an attention-seeker. But I owe my personality and career to my childhood. It made me into the social person I am today. Throughout my whole life, my papa, who is ninety years young now, always called me two names. It was either, "Tony, you character…" or "Tony, such an actor you are…" in his deep Sicilian voice. I really was, though. I met so many people while growing up, and at times had to adapt when making new friends in another new city and school. I may have had to act a different way, maybe learn new hobbies that were more popular in that area.

At the end of the day, I am fortunate it gave me the social personality I have today. I think that's what brought me to real estate. It became a habit to not be comfortable, to always want to meet new people, make new friends, and in real estate, that's the key to being successful. Whether you are a real estate agent reading this book, financial broker, insurance agent, business owner, attorney, salesperson, musician, entrepreneur, entertainer, fashion designer, etc., you are probably a "people person" as much as I am, and I'm sure you realize your profession is a contact sport. Isn't any profession? The goal in these and so many more businesses is to reach people, clients, fans, followers, etc.

In the last few years we have watched the global economy in crisis; however, we have all witnessed the industry of social media explode into a multi-billion-dollar empire! Why is social media so profitable and gaining steam more and more every day? The reason is simply that it is not just a MySpace page for a college student anymore. Social media is a world within itself—in fact, nothing has ever grown at a faster rate than the world's population until Facebook. The crazy thing is this is just the beginning, but the most common mistake made is assuming that 'if you build it, they will come' works in social networking. It does not...

bio

Tony Giordano was born and raised in Southern California. Growing up, his passion and goals were to become a firefighter, which he became in the year 2000 after graduating from the academy. In the years leading up to that, he enjoyed life-guarding, first-aid teaching, getting his EMT certification, and being a part of the sheriff's Search and Rescue Team. However, while in school, he was always attracted to the business world. He loved math, finance, and real estate in general. So as a reserve firefighter, he decided to study and enter the mortgage industry, becoming a top producer with many banking institutions. But he wanted that knowledge to eventually prep him to enter the real estate sales side of the industry. Tony now currently sells real estate with one of the largest companies in the world. He started in the real estate industry in 1998, developing a vast knowledge of all aspects of the industry: lending, insurance, development, residential, commercial, etc. In recent years he focused on adapting within the industry by being trained in social media. This training has given him a massive advantage on his competition. It has also allowed him to build his own relocation network around the world as a real estate professional. In addition to real estate, he is now a social media consultant, guest speaker, and author to help teach companies, universities, and/or business executives how to 'correctly' integrate social media in their business.

start social networking

Social Network:*: is a social structure made up of individuals (or organizations) called "nodes," which are tied (connected) by one or more specific types of interdependency, such as friendship, kinship, common interest, financial exchange, dislike, sexual relationships, or relationships of beliefs, knowledge, or prestige (Wikipedia).*

So what is a social agent? In real estate, there is no better way to describe it. It's who we are or what we need to be, and now social media is making it even easier. But it's not just realtors; it works for everyone in business. You can be the social executive, the social salesperson, the social insurance agent, the social banker, the social attorney, the social doctor, the social business owner, the social mechanic, etc. It's the same philosophy and it works equally.

With the 'New Era of Social Networking' it has brought us the new era of 'forward slash // follow me' with almost everything now. What do I mean by that? Well, if it doesn't come to your mind right offhand, I would like to give you a hint and also my info...feel free to contact me via:

Add me www.Facebook.com/TonyGiordano.info
Follow me www.Twitter.com/SocialAgentBook
Subscribe me www.youtube.com/tonygiordano23
Connect me www.linkedin.com/pub/tony-giordano/20/1/263

That right there is the "New Era of Forward Slash // Follow Me": my company, my music, my art, my ideas. It is social networking and it is here to stay. Now with hundreds of millions of users on all these social media networks, you may already have this first chapter down since you may already be on a few. But it's always fun to educate new ones and to remind the veterans how it all started and what we did in the beginning. For me personally, it all started with my personal MySpace page in 2007. I know, not that long ago, right? But think about that: three years later, I am consulting and writing a book on it. The reason is I went from not being serious about it to being very serious once I saw it work and increase my business. Facebook played a key role in this. I went through the correct training, read a bunch on the topic, and actually did what the instructors told me to do. Then I learned some great things on my own and started realizing it worked in other ways that I came up with.

In the words of my first social media trainer, Joshua Patz, "Ok, why don't we begin with the 'Fab 5'?"

Facebook, Twitter, LinkedIn, Google+, & YouTube. These networks are by far the largest in the world, and even as other networks rise, the 'Fab 5' are the key networks and work the best, period. This will keep you from wondering which ones to use out of the hundreds to choose from. It will also keep you from going insane trying to manage dozens of networks that you will not see many benefits from.

● ● ●

why Facebook?

Facebook (FB) is not a profile, like it originally started as for college students. It has come a long way. A quick glimpse at years it took to reach 50 million people: radio—38 years, TV—13 years, Internet—4 years, Ipod—3 years, and Facebook...? Try 100 million people in 9 months, 200 MILLION in 12 months! Is it a FAD? Or the biggest shift since the industrial revolution? Some go further by saying it's the largest fundamental shift in the way we communicate in history! If you have a moment, search a video on YouTube titled 'Social Media Revolution.' These are short videos created by Eric Qualman, author of the book Socialnomics. Your jaw will drop with how many compelling statistics it shows. (There are a few versions of the video.)

Facebook as a whole with its profiles, pages, marketplace, ads, and the hundreds of networks for companies, schools, etc. is massive pools of people around the globe in the hundreds of millions. There is no end in sight to Facebook being in the billions soon enough. Probably by the time I finish writing this book. Facebook's technology and its size is the example of what all other networks are striving for. If you don't have one, feel free to take a break right now and create your page—seriously, it's very easy. Or you can read the book once and then read it again next to your computer or tablet.

Facebook does change things from time to time, but always for the better. The new Facebook Timeline profile truly is a sign of the future and really does create a digital identity for you in an era when you must have one (now!). We live in a digital world where we are 'Googled' before we get the call.

• • •

why Twitter?

Twitter is a way to know the news without waiting for it. It's not just following your favorite celebrities and knowing when they are at Starbucks. It's about communication and self-expression. No matter what you do, you can search for it. Think about your profession when I give you this example of mine. I, as a real estate agent, can search on Twitter the words "looks like I'm relocating to Los Angeles soon" and it will then pull up every 'tweet' where those words are used. I then scroll down and find one that seems to be serious and then @mention the individual, simply offering my expertise on the market and schools to help them learn about the area when they are looking for a home. Do you get it? Don't you think I now may have a better shot of earning their business or at least am working on more quality leads? There are also what are called popular trends that Twitter will post. These are words or phrases with a # (hashtag) in front of them that are being tweeted by millions. You can use it however you want and you will get followers by doing so. Example: Twitter shows in the 'trends' #WhereAreTheyNow and millions will be using this in their tweets differently. For me, I will tweet, 'Buyers are starting to look for homes, #WhereAreTheyNow? Let me find you a home!' Sometimes after using a trend like this, you will get alerts of new people following you. Fun, right? Twitter has risen as one of the top social networks because it works. It took Twitter 16 months to reach 600,000 users, and now just a few years later, it has about 600,000 new users a day!

● ● ●

why LinkedIn?

LinkedIn is pretty much the business professional network. On this site it is very easy to stay connected to any and all since most have a LinkedIn profile. This site allows you to recruit for your company, meet potential clients...you can even find out the name and info of practically any CEO of any company in the world. Think about that for a second. You can use LinkedIn for so many different things but here's one example: if I heard that a corporation out of New York was either opening or closing a division in LA, and obviously there will be executives transferring as well as new hires, now I can go on LinkedIn, search for people of Company A, and start connecting. Let them know that I am there to answer questions and help in any way I can. Who do you think will be their agent?

A very well known LinkedIn genius, is a good friend of mine by the name of Lewis Howes. He has helped thousands gain business from LinkedIn by approaching it correctly. Lewis says, "LinkedIn is the most powerful business networking site on the planet. With the highest average household income over any other major social networking site, and nearly 45% of users being business decision makers, it's the number one place you should be spending your time when wanting to attract the best leads for your business." www.LewisHowes.com I think we would all agree why LinkedIn is part of the Fab-5.

● ● ●

why YouTube?

In this book, there is a chapter that will discuss the importance of video marketing, video connecting, and how video is the new way to search, track, and market. Why? Well, in a world now where 2 billion videos are viewed yearly—yes, 2 billion videos are watched yearly—it is vital to make yourself known in any profession. For myself, if someone Googles 'Los Angeles real estate' or anything for that matter, have you noticed how videos pop up at the top of the page? Those are videos on YouTube or video sites that have key words and titles common to what you searched. I don't know about you, but I would rather watch a video real quick than read, and I'm not alone. Even more powerful is the new YouTube interface that is launching which truly creates the perfect combination of video and social networking. Everyone will be switched over to the new interface as the year moves forward. This is why adapting to video is key in your business.

● ● ●

why Google+?

Google owns YouTube, which is the second-largest search engine in the world now. Who's first? Google is... so of course it makes sense to have a Google+ profile. This is the newest social network but with the power of the Google name and the millions who already have gmail accounts and profiles, it is very easy for the network to already be in the FAB 5. It makes you separate yourself from your competition and makes it easier for people to find you. Let's say your name is John Smith... pretty common name here in the U.S., right? Well, if someone happened to hear your name or see your name as an expert in your field and 'Googled' it real quick, how many do you think would show up? Same profession and even the same area, too? But if you had a YouTube channel and a Google+ profile, how easy do you think it would be for them to view yours first and contact you? Let me just say: easy! So create your profile asap and go put some people in your various Google+ 'circles,' as they call them.

You will notice right out of the gate that the different networks have different names for the action of connecting with someone. Everybody wants to be different, right? ☺ As with anything, start with your warm market, your friends, family, and co-workers...you know they love us for it. ☺ You will probably be shocked how many of them have a Facebook, Twitter, etc. account. Add them on Facebook, follow their Twitter and get them to follow you back, connect with them professionally on LinkedIn, subscribe to their YouTube channel, put them in a circle on Google+, etc.

Now with a personal Facebook profile, it is VERY important to start creating groups (Create Lists) as soon as you start adding friends; the reason for this is as you create your network, if you are not grouping at the beginning when you only have 300 people, imagine later when you have 3000 and you have to go to each person one by one and place them in a list because you never took the time at the beginning to create lists like family, friends, associates, acquaintances, etc. FYI: Google+ makes this task very easy on their profile with their 'circles.'

Tip—Learn from the FAQs on the various sites!!!

There is a reason these sites and networks are almost impossible to call on the phone; they have worked very hard to list the answer to almost any question you could possibly have. FAQs really come across as a virtual instructor to learn from and help you 24/7. The problem is no one ever tries to learn from them because people still think of the old-school FAQs that were always the same questions and answers on any website and never were the questions you wanted answered. That has changed, and for the better!

Tip—Learn the BASIC privacy settings immediately!!!

The basic privacy settings are your best friend. Your most important initial task, in my opinion, is to immediately make a simple setting under Privacy to not allow people to tag you in photos or videos; this will help you breathe a little bit until you learn the advanced settings later in the book. You can't get scared about people knowing or seeing your basic info. *I hate to be the one to tell you, but anyone can know anything these days, so you might as well adapt and let them know you correctly. Remember, you control who you are; you control your information.*

Tip—Take a beginner social media networking class!!!

The reason I am constantly out there teaching classes when I'm not selling property is people want to see you show them, they want to see the navigation tasks, the do's and the do not's. Classes will help you retain what you're learning a little better. As I continue traveling and consulting, I have learned that most large companies will provide them for their employees. This is another indication that social media is not going anywhere and is changing the game forever. Classes are a fast, inexpensive way of seeing the instructor actually direct you in person and help you navigate throughout the pages and sites.

You can also search almost any social media question on YouTube and watch a video on how to do something; that makes it very easy. We will discuss this later in more detail.

Aside from your warm market of friends, family, and associates, now start to Like, Follow, Connect, and Subscribe to everything YOU want and have interests in. For example: liking a page on FB (Facebook) now gives you the ability in most cases to tag them in a post, where whoever runs their social media can sometimes see it depending on the type of page they have. Genius, in my opinion! Don't worry, we will discuss correct ways to tag later in the book. ☺ This works on Twitter as well, for example: following someone on Twitter now at least keeps you in touch with them and their tweets as well as @mentioning, which they will see, too. Even if they don't follow you back, they can see when you re-tweet their posts or @mention them in your own tweet (@mentions are also explained later). ☺

Aside from these reasons, liking, following, subscribing, circling, etc. allows and opens the door to having interests in common with other people and contacts. The more you have in common, the easier it is to connect and/or be suggested to connect—for example, when Facebook tells you that you may know this individual for that particular common reason or mutual friend. Pretty cool, right?

Well, that takes care of some of the initial networks and tasks to focus on. Let's start having a little fun now. Our next chapter goes into the speed increase of your business when using the engine of social media...

Personal Notes & Ideas

. . . .
. . . .
. . . .
. . . .
. . . .
. . . .
. . . .
. . . .
. . . .
. . . .
. . . .
. . . .
. . . .
. . . .
. . . .
. . . .
. . . .

CHAPTER 2

social speedia

If you are too busy for social media, then you are TOO busy... It's like saying you're too busy to say hi to someone on the street. Or too busy when you are introduced to someone to say "hi" vs. "sorry, I'm too busy to meet any more people on earth." Personally when I hear someone say this who actually needs it in their business, I consider it an excuse. It makes me want to sit down with them right there and show them the speed and ease of it. For those who say they are too busy, social media can actually free up your time. But enough about them...we're learning something here! ☺

"From a national brand level, social media opens doors of communication like nothing else. It gives you the ability to have thousands of one-on-one conversations with your clients at any given moment." *David Marine, Coldwell Banker, Director, Consumer Experience*

You also need to realize that with every new time-consuming task, one old one is usually replaced. If social media is quickly taking on the entire role in communication, networking, marketing, information, and advertising, then it's taking a huge load off the time we spent on all those things separately. Make sense? I no longer have to chase all these tasks down; they are all in one place today.

When the Internet, faxing, and emailing blew up, yeah, it was time-consuming for people to learn, understand, and adapt to them, but didn't that replace the time of letter-writing, messenger services, having to research all day long at a library for info? The key is you had to adapt, and the ones who did benefited the most.

At first, yes, it may seem too time-consuming learning the basics; it was for me. But I quickly got over that when only after a few weeks I saw it work and got business from it. Like anything, it gets easier with practice, just like any new task in business, whether it's door-knocking, cold-calling, writing, networking, and our favorite as sales professionals: BSing (lol)!

Most agents, sales execs, and business professionals already find themselves in front of a computer or on the go with a smart mobile device every day. These devices make it extremely simple today to adapt to change. We have the world's info at our fingertips at any point of the day. Applications on phones started as games and fun time-killers; however, now applications take the role of a mini version of a desktop website. The Facebook app does mostly everything the website does, but it makes it easier so you can navigate on your smart phone; same with Twitter, YouTube, and so on. In addition to apps, we have also seen the explosion of QR codes, which are like UPC bar codes. You've seen them…they are square and look like mini crossword puzzles. Well, with these codes, smart-phone users download a QR reader application, then when you see this code, you take a picture of it and it takes you directly to the website, advertisement, picture, whatever the code is supposed to be used for in that particular ad. Make sure when you start to use these in your ads that they don't just go to your website, where people then have to take the time to navigate through it, which,

most times, is not easy if you do not have a mobile-friendly website. QR codes are for on the go, so if you are using one, say, for a property listing of yours, make sure it goes directly to the listing, otherwise it will not serve its purpose. If you have a smart phone and do not have this QR reader app, stop reading and download it real quick. Then scan this QR image on the left...

Pretty cool, right?

Remember, technology is always evolving and it's always dominating the technology before it by being faster, superior, and smarter! Shouldn't you be faster, superior, and smarter than your competition?

Nonetheless, there are many tools and sites that do the work for you now. Take, for instance, hootSuite.com; this site is free and great! Although I believe you get more if you pay a small monthly fee, the gist is that this site manages your social media sites if you want it to. It creates a banner at the top of your desktop screen where you can type in something you want to share on Facebook, Twitter, or wherever, and hootsuite.com automatically posts it to all the sites for you. Now you have no excuse! You can also set it up to post different things at different times for you throughout the day in case you will be away from doing it yourself, maybe on vacation, golfing, a seminar...whatever.

I often come back from a long day when I didn't have any time to share my thoughts or post content, and have dozens of alerts and comments on posts that day because I forgot I had set my posts up in the morning. Facebook has now rolled out a planner app that allows you to schedule your FB posts in advance, which I'm sure the other social networks will follow as well.

Interns can also be a great asset. That's right, you are important enough to have your own college intern. Interns are almost always college students who want to learn your particular business, which may also be their major. They get extra credit and are sometimes advised by teachers to look into these positions locally. Interns and students are the up-and-coming generation of business executives and business owners. I have learned from interns just as much as they have learned from me.

Did you know that the vast majority of the next generation between the ages of 13 and 23 do not have traditional email accounts and, if they do, do not use them to communicate regularly? What do you think they are using to communicate? You got it: SOCIAL MEDIA.

These same kids are also the brains that started social media, remember? They are the next generation of your clients. I will say that again: these kids and young adults are your future clients. They are doctors, attorneys, public officers, bankers, etc.

In regards to the individuals who are pursuing your line of work, be nervous if you don't adapt and integrate social media today. For the first time ever, rookie professionals who understand this social media industry can and will take the business of a veteran professional tomorrow. I, along with many I have educated on social media, are living proof.

Personal Notes & Ideas

. . . .

. . . .

. . . .

. . . .

. . . .

. . . .

. . . .

. . . .

. . . .

. . . .

. . . .

. . . .

. . . .

. . . .

. . . .

. . . .

. . . .

lights, camera, action...

action: *Organized activity to accomplish an objective*

As social media has risen in the last few years, so has video on the Internet. Now more than ever, companies are realizing the importance of video marketing and video direction. As an effort to embrace new technology, large corporations are hiring companies like Rep Interactive, a premiere video agency of record (VOAR) company, to produce video content year round. If large businesses are doing this, don't you think it's a good time to consider it for your small business?

YouTube is the second-largest search engine in the world. If you take a second and think about that, it means people are searching for anything on YouTube with the hope they can watch a video on it. We aren't talking about searching new music videos and funny kids coming home from the dentist. Anything and everything is searched for on YouTube now. People search videos to find real estate, insurance, financial services, cars, boats, etc. They search for 'how to do' videos. People would much rather watch a video on 'how to,' let's say, fix their computer than to read directions or an article. Recently I was trying to locate the hard drive on a laptop of mine. I Googled it, which then showed a bunch of web results of tech sites to read blogs or answers from individuals. I tried to read and understand what they were saying but it was not working. Then I remembered my own philosophy of video. So I clicked 'video' in the results page, which then took me straight to Youtube, where I pressed play and it showed someone with the exact laptop turn it over, grab a screwdriver, take a section off, then press a button, and out popped the hard drive, all in 30 seconds! Kind of like when we were kids we always wanted to watch the movie to do our book reports! ☺

It has been reported that 51% of all online content viewed is video content (_Wired Magazine-The Web is Dead)._

There are now 2 billion videos watched online a year, which is twice as much as the year before. Video has truly taken over. An estimated 56% of affluent Internet users have watched a YouTube video in the last 24 hours (_Jan 2011 survey done by L2 Agency)._

Tablets like the iPad have only made video-watching even easier on the go. There has been a 400% increase in time spent watching video by iPad users vs. web users (_Source Mefeedia)._

The only thing stopping you from appearing larger-than-life is your online presence. With statistics like this, it is time to create your own YouTube channel. I know some of you may be hesitant in creating a channel because you may not have made videos yet. A little trick is to, at first, upload to your channel some great videos in your profession that are already on YouTube. Nothing wrong with that, and it will give you some initial content while you are working on your own videos. Maybe your company has videos and commercials they have done. I know my company does, so upload some from your industry to your channel.

When you are ready to start, record 30-60-second videos. You want to try to keep videos to a minute, max. Reason being studies have shown that viewers tend to lose interest after 60 seconds on average, unless it continues to intrigue and is fast-moving. There may be a little nervousness on your side initially talking into the camera for a change. Don't worry, it goes away; you must power through it. Most of us in individual branding and sales have a natural talent when it comes to this. Actors and salespeople have very much in common. I like to stare at the camera and imagine a friend or client's face when I am talking. Helps me stay focused and remember my script. Whether you're in real estate or ANY profession, video marketing is extremely important and works when done correctly and professionally.

You know when you search Google for something, videos always seem to be at the top of the results page? Well, that's what I mean: everything is tracked by video now online. There is no question, for me, 90% of the time I will watch the video on the topic before going to website results.

Example: someone in Australia searches for Los Angeles real estate, and the results page pops up all of these different real estate sites; however, there are also a couple videos that are at the top of the page. So they press play, and it's a real estate agent with a sharp, professionally done video talking about and showing video on Los Angeles. At the end of the video it shows his or her website. Now the buyer from Australia has a REASON to go to your website and contact you. This works in all fields; this same example could have been an insurance agent, mechanic, stock broker, attorney...the list goes on and on.

Anyone in sales should have a promo video of themselves that can be posted on the web. It is critical to hire a professional video agency for your promo video on who you are and not cut corners. You don't want it to look cheap; do your clients think you look cheap when they meet you? Then why would you want your video to look cheap? This is a major investment in yourself and your business. While some people and companies spend upwards of $25,000 on their videos, there is a wide range of cost, but I would suggest budgeting a few thousand to do it right. Remember, this will be the online extension of yourself FOREVER. You cannot afford to look bad with poor quality. Your goal is to want to be able to craft an excellent wordpress website and have a cinema-quality video commercial for yourself and your business. Think movie trailer about you. This will set you far above your competition and the thousands of similar promo videos out there that just don't seem to capture attention. Spend some money and reap the rewards.

Now you don't have to hire a company every time; there are many times I grab my smart phone and will shoot a quick 30-second video of a new listing of mine or an update on the market, and although it may seem distorted and shaky, it's just another video uploaded to my YouTube channel. You only need one cinema-quality video of yourself like the kind REP Interactive produced for me. Here is an example of mine:

Hope you enjoyed that... ☺

There are many real estate video companies like ehome tours that will also shoot professional video of your listing for about $200. These are great supplements that follow your smart phone videos and they work well for marketing properties. However, keep in mind that your promo video must be cinema or movie standard quality because it's used as an online projection of who you are. A first impression per se in a new day and age where online networking has taken over.

Just as you want to create content on social media sites, you want to do the same on video sites. Upload videos whenever you can. There are plenty of video websites that you want your videos on as well. Not just YouTube. Now I know you're probably thinking, *How am I going to find the time to upload videos on all these different video sites besides YouTube?* No worries. There are sites like TubeMogul.com that, once you upload it there, the site will upload it automatically to a dozen video sites if you want it to.

When uploading and creating a title for your video, you want to identify and use the right key words to tag the video with. Make sure your titles reflect what people are searching for and/or how you would search for that video. The goal is to be on the first page of results when someone searches. Google analytics are very helpful in showing the right keywords and ones commonly used... just search 'Google analytics' and it's very self-explanatory.

I would like to take a second and let you hear some directions and tips from one of the best video companies out there. Steve Gatena is the founder and CEO of REP Interactive LLC, a premiere online agency that specializes in video and interactive media. REP Interactive is based in Southern California and began as an academic research project at the University of Southern California. Steve played football at USC and shortly after winning the 2009 Rose Bowl, he decided to begin researching online video. As part of his master's thesis, Gatena focused on the effects online video marketing had on the residential and commercial real estate industries. Gatena and his classmate Andy McNeil began REP Interactive as a way to conduct research while working on their thesis project. Guided by market research, academic theory, and clinical experiments, Gatena and McNeil developed a formula for viral videos and effective marketing videos. They also invented a strategic method for creating engaging, entertaining, informative, and motivational pieces that had higher retention ratings and less viewer dropout. To see an example of their work, Google "Most Expensive Homes in the World" and their video will come up first. This video was one of their thesis videos in 2010 and it is the most viewed real estate video in North America. REP Interactive got all those views without spending a dime and without using any celebrities.

Gatena and McNeil have grown REP Interactive into a full-service video agency that now works with clients like Coldwell Banker, Marriott, GE Healthcare, CBRE, Los Angeles Dodgers, and more.

Here is what Steve and his team have to say about the importance of video marketing in business: ***"VIDEO IS THE***

MOST IMPORTANT THING EVER!" That could be a bit of an overstatement, but he has some great points that can't easily be argued with. Much of this advice has benefited me greatly and increased my business and online presence substantially. Steve says,

"With today's advanced technology, video is the number one method for connecting to your potential clients. Long gone are the days of one-to-one communication. One-to-one is where one person can communicate with one person at a time. Examples of one-to-one communication are meeting people in person or talking to one other person via telephone. Now that we have the ability to communicate in a one-to-many format, it is important that you take advantage of that. With one video, you can connect with millions of people online. What other tool can do that for you? Could you imagine the possibilities and opportunities that would be created if you posted a video about yourself or your business and 5,000 people saw it? What if 500,000 people saw it? Or 5,000,000? How many of those could become potential clients or create a recommendation for you to other potential clients?

Whether you choose to use video as a live-environment selling tool to present property or simply make a personal introduction, first impressions are everything. Sophisticated advancements in mobile technology and high-speed Internet allow you to genuinely and intimately communicate with people around the world. Now you can interactively present value propositions, virtually demonstrate your brand strengths, and digitally educate your viewers faster and more effectively than ever before. The statistics are there; right now video is the real deal and if you're not using it you're already behind.

So we know video is important and that it can help. What are some other important video facts we should keep in mind? Video in and of itself does not deliver positive results.

You need a great video and fantastic distribution. Bad video is extremely detrimental to your entire enterprise. It's just like real life: horrible presentations don't exactly convey a sense of confidence and trust in consumers, right? On the other hand, excellent presentations that are genuine and to the point can provide tremendous results. Treat your primary business video like the commercial for your political campaign. It has to sum up all of your strengths, present you and your business in a confident and positive manner, and leave the viewer wanting to endorse you. It is very difficult to find professionals that can help you execute these goals effectively. You have got to work with someone who has experience. Here are some key questions you should ask a video agency before choosing to hire them:

- ☐ *Do you have an online portfolio of work and can you please send me some pieces you have created in addition to referrals or endorsements of your work? A company should always have an online portfolio and they should be able to send you dozens of pieces of work. If they cannot, you should move on and select another company.*
- ☐ *What companies do you typically work with and what is your role when working with these organizations? As you know, a client list is important. Equally important is the role a company plays for their clients and the level of participation companies have on projects. You want to find a company that really gets their hands dirty and works on campaigns from the ground up.*
- ☐ *Do you craft creative concepts, write scripts, and choose locations or are you the type of video company that shows up with cameras and waits for direction from me? Just because someone knows*

how to operate a camera and a Macbook doesn't mean they are qualified to create your online persona. You want a company of experts that will guide you every step of the way and not leave major duties on your plate.

☐ Do you have any strategic partnerships with companies like Google or YouTube that can help me distribute my video or run a video campaign? Only some of the top video agencies in the world have these partnerships. Just because an agency is not associated with these companies does not mean they do not produce good work, although acquiring a YouTube partnership and, more importantly, a Google partnership allows you to do a number of exceptional distribution tactics that are not available to those without these partnerships. Also, the official stamp of approval from these two organizations is likely a great indicator that the company you are dealing with is legitimate.

☐ Can you create a plan to guarantee my video is viewed by others? The best answer here is, 'We cannot guarantee views. However, we have created a variety of successful distribution campaigns that have helped our clients achieve success.' No company can guarantee views. However, there are tactics that can be used that work a majority of the time. Distributing videos effectively takes time and costs money. Set a standard of success for your video, be it a number of views online, a number of leads generated, or some desired positive reactions. Discuss these standards openly with your video agency and ask them how their plan will achieve the standards you are in search of.

☐ How long should my video be? Why? YOUR VIDEO SHOULD NEVER BE LONGER THAN 2 MINUTES.

We recommend 60 seconds or less. If a company tells you that they will make you a video that's four to five minutes long, you should ask them why and if they have any facts that show that will be effective.

☐ *What will I be required to do to help the process? Know what you are getting yourself into. You are a busy person; writing treatments, scripts, shots lists, choosing locations, creating legal documents for releases, applying for permits, and designing sets is extremely difficult. If you hire the wrong company, they might just show up with a set of cameras, no plan, and expect that you have done all the work.*

Always keep in mind, although you are not a video expert, nobody knows your business, your customer, and yourself better than you. Try to find a great video company to work with that can act as an expert consultant and collaborative partner. Building your online persona takes time, money, and should never be haphazardly constructed. It requires a team of experts and your industry knowledge. Most importantly, it should be an extremely fun and exciting process, so have a blast doing it!"

I'm sure you agree with Steve after reading about his experiences and profession. So what are you waiting for? It is time to play the lead role in your own True Hollywood story. You are the star and you can beat your competition by being up-to-date with video marketing. Educate on your videos just as you do on the social network sites. Be a reason for people to want to subscribe to your channel. See, here you thought your childhood aspirations of being an actor or actress came and went...no, they didn't. Ready, TAKE I...

Personal Notes & Ideas

· ·

· ·

· ·

· ·

· ·

· ·

· ·

· ·

· ·

· ·

· ·

· ·

· ·

· ·

· ·

· ·

gated community (privacy 101)

Every time I guest-speak or consult on social media, I always get the same first question, "What if I don't want my info and pictures for everyone to see, especially my business associates?" Don't let the public viewing aspect of social media deter you.

Your clients and business associates want to learn more about you. That's why you have them as clients—they like you! What if they invited you to their home for a get-together; wouldn't you present yourself well and keep manners in mind? Well, it's the same with social media now. It didn't start that way, but like it or not, it is the fastest-growing gateway to our social lives; you have to embrace it. Not that long ago it seemed cool to not have a MySpace or Facebook, but now in a weird way, if you don't have a social network, it's the opposite effect; now people think you're trying to hide something. Obviously not always the case for people who don't, but it's an ever-growing observation I am seeing now. I have several friends who, a couple years ago and even a few months ago, told me, "I will never be on Facebook, Twitter, etc..." and now not only do they have them, but are on them every day socially and professionally.

Whether you are new to social networking or consider yourself technically advanced and choose not to be on a social network because of your privacy preferences, you will be eventually. There really are not many reasons that make sense not to anymore, mainly due to secure settings now and that it has grown from a fun thing to do to an addition to who we are as a person.

Example: Mr. A is a very private person and likes to keep business and his personal life separate. The time is 10 years ago, let's say, and he is invited over to a new client's home for a party they are throwing because they want to get to know him better. He knows their friends will be there and is looking forward to networking and maybe getting some more business, too. Mr. A makes sure to dress nice, grabs some of his business cards, and heads over to the party. He is greeted at the door and welcomed in, but his clients notice that Mr. A seems to be acting strange, a bit too serious. They are trying to get him to unwind but everything seems to be business with him. All the other people are dancing, taking pictures, laughing, and just being social without a care in the world, but there is Mr. A, in the corner, not wanting to show his social side. He met some new people, passed some cards out, made sure to thank his new clients for the invite, and although he 'may' hear from his clients again, he pretty much has already been forgotten by everyone else the next day.

Do you see where I am going with this? Friends, this example is happening every minute now online. This is how people are staying in touch more than with any other form of communication or social scene. You DO NOT want to be Mr. A in the corner.

It is very easy, say, on Facebook to make picture albums on a private setting and other albums on a public setting. You can even control who can post on your walls. Twitter is already very private; it is mainly a site of communication and staying in tune with things that interest you and not having to worry about people emailing you and sending you messages if you do not follow them back on Twitter. Even your video uploads to your YouTube channel can have privacy settings.

Learn how to customize your advanced privacy settings. I call them advanced because they take a little deeper digging to set them and find them. There are the quick basic settings you may already have set, like we previously discussed. Then you will learn the advanced ones. FAQs will show you answers to privacy questions, but just as the previous chapters discussed, who wants to read through questions and dialogue? Just simply search on YouTube for instructions. Try it: right now, pull up YouTube and search, for example, 'How to Make a Facebook Picture Album Private.' You will be able to sit back and watch someone do it, which makes it very easy to then do it yourself. In my opinion, I see FAQs in the future actually being videos on these sites. You will just click the FAQs, let's say on Google+, and then it will automatically start playing a YouTube video. Why not? Remember, you heard it here first. ☺

In this book you will learn the importance of 'Grouping' (Creating Lists) of your friends on Facebook, or 'Circles' on Google+; that's when privacy settings get fun. You can have a family group, friends group, business group, etc. Then let's say you want one group to not know your religious views, maybe you don't want your business group to know your political preference or relationship status, etc. When you go to post something on your FB wall, have you ever noticed the little padlock to the left of the Share button? Press the lock first and it will let you customize which people will be able to see the post you're about to make; if you're going to be expressing yourself in a manner not suitable for Mom and Dad or business associates, simply lock them out—it really is that easy. But, again, simply YouTube it and watch a video on how to create lists or any type of groups and settings.

That is why I named this chapter what I did, not just for my fellow real estate agents, but, just like a gated community with a security guard, you give friends and family the 'gate code,' per se. Everyone else has to check in to security and call the house. It's simple and easy to be private on any of these social networks.

Tip—It's okay to not play 'Tag, you're it!'

Remember, you control your pages, and just as I have done in the past, it's okay to tell friends and family not to tag you just as you tell them personal things in life and ask them not to share it, right? Social media is the new way we communicate; it's the new way we express ourselves on the go. The same rules with human relationships still apply.

Now, you can simply set your privacy settings to make it so no one can tag you in photos, but their friends can still see a picture of you on their profile; they just won't see your name. You will also see that on Facebook, if you set your privacy settings to not allow friends and contacts to tag you in photos, it means they can't tag you in videos as well. Facebook doesn't separate photos and videos to have a setting each, and since I am tagged in professional videos frequently, I allow myself to be tagged in photos, too. However, I have my notification settings set to text my phone when I'm tagged and I can immediately remove the tag if I was having a bad hair day. ☺ But remember, the people who tag you in photos are usually your closest friends and family who you can simply ask not to tag you. The latest positive move with tagging on Facebook is that they finally rolled out the option to approve anything you are tagged in. If you enable this 'approval' setting then you do not have to worry about anything we just discussed above because you now approve or ignore any tag, whether a post, picture, video, etc.

Personal Notes & Ideas

. . . .

. . . .

. . . .

. . . .

. . . .

. . . .

. . . .

. . . .

. . . .

. . . .

. . . .

. . . .

. . . .

. . . .

. . . .

. . . .

. . . .

one word: adaptability

Adaptability: *The ability to change (or be changed) to fit changed circumstances*

In real estate and any profession, when you think about it, there is one word that perfectly describes what we all need to have. Many use other words, but I have always thought this one was the best...

Someone recently asked me, "Tony, what are your thoughts on Social Security?" I replied humorously, "I think it is very important to have a Facebook account..." It seems I have adapted to such a point that I only think about social media when I hear the word "social."

See, the great ones are great because they don't get "comfortable," in my opinion. There is that word again—comfortable—but really think about this word. What happens when we are comfortable in life, let's say relaxing on a sunny day, right? We find our lounge chair, grab a book, and get comfortable. This means we don't want to change anything at that moment. Of course not! We realize that no one is going to take that away from us; we can stay as long as the sun stays up. Well, in business, this word is not the same, because while we are comfortable loving our current business, income is good, and just no reason to change anything, guess what? Someone is already working on taking your business right from under your nose. Why? Because they change constantly, they adapt, and they always think about the future. They choose not to be comfortable in business, so they can truly be comfortable in life. I am not saying working all the time and never taking a break. I am saying adapting to new ways of doing business that are almost always making business tasks easier. Social media and technology have given us not just the opportunity to meet new people but be more mobile and still get all our work done, leaving more time for family, friends, and clients.

Change with the times:

- ☐ Do you have a website?
- ☐ Do you have email?
- ☐ Do have a smart phone?
- ☐ Do you even have a phone?
- ☐ Do you have a fax?
- ☐ Do you have a tablet?

Do you see where this is going? You have already changed with the times from the competition before you, and them before theirs. Imagine if you didn't have the forms of technology mentioned above in your business today. Well, that is exactly what they will be saying about social media in the future, and, in all honesty, they already are. Nearly 90% of real estate buyers come directly from the Internet now!

This goes for almost all forms of business. I hear it all the time, whether I'm teaching real estate agents, the auto industry, brokerage firms, insurance, product supply, etc. They all say that the amount of customers for their line of work coming from the Internet now has increased substantially. The Internet is who we

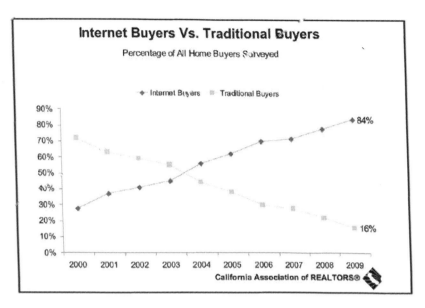

Internet Buyers Vs. Traditional Buyers
Percentage of All Home Buyers Surveyed

◆ Internet Buyers ▪ Traditional Buyers

California Association of REALTORS®

are and how we find information, but information also finds us now. That is due to the fact that the Internet has changed. It has evolved to the rise of social media. It has made us change the way we used to surf it to the way we surf it now, and the way it benefits the world of business.

Door-knocking and open houses CAN'T compete with the web and social media, they just can't! Yes, you may get a new client here and there, but it can't even come close to the scale and dominance of social networks. Just as any old form of networking and marketing can't compete with a new way that reaches the masses. Yes, past forms of advertising, marketing and networking still work on some level. Of course. But that is the key word, on "some" level. The graph on the next page is almost identical in all fields of business. I don't have to tell you where your focus should be.

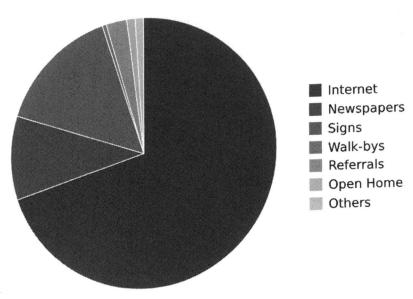

Google Images 2011

It was only a few years ago that you had to do an open house and spend a ton of money on print ads in magazines when marketing a home for sale. These reached hundreds, maybe thousands, on a local level. Now you post a listing on social networks and websites that get millions of visits a month, and just like news finds us today, listings find buyers who don't realize they are buyers.

So the question remains: whether you are a 40-year veteran or a 3-year veteran, have you changed? There is one individual who hopes you are not changing or adapting, and that individual is the rookie who just got a job in your industry and understands the power of social media. It would be equal to a company 15 years ago having a website, fax, and email system compared to a competitor who did not.

Here is an example of when I first realized the power of social media. I may have been a veteran agent in the real estate industry, but that does not mean I was the best or most productive in volume. So this same example would have worked if I had been a rookie, without question. For this story I will leave the name of the agent out and we will call him Frank B, who was the top #1 agent for the area.

I got a call from a lady who was thinking about listing her beachfront home in Southern California. The client spared no time in telling me, "I also have already interviewed Frank B for the listing." Always nice to hear that, right? Lol! Well, since we are all 'people' people, we love the challenge of sales and the business. I proceeded to tell her about me and how I would approach the sale of her home. She asked me to come by the house and take a look, so we met for an hour or so and I gave her my listing presentation on my iPad, which she very much enjoyed and thought it was a very modern way of presenting. She loved how it allowed her to actually be a part of it herself. Now, in the old days, that was it: Frank B, who is #1, and I both got a meeting and listing presentation in her living room and both would be following up with emails and thank-you notes, may the best agent win. Wrong! Introducing Exhibit A: Facebook! The seller and I met, we laughed, she invited me into her home, so why not add her as a friend? She has the right to say no, but in this case she accepted my request. What did I just do? I just turned a one-hour listing presentation into a presentation every day until she decides which agent she's going with. She now sees posts about other clients of mine, properties I have recently sold and posted about, and she knows basic info about my life, things I enjoy, family...and that means your potential clients realize that you want to get to know them and stay in touch. Personally, I enjoy becoming friends with my clients and, needless to say, I got the listing two weeks later.

Social media has changed the game, and if business and sales have always been a contact sport, then adapt and start connecting with the new ways we have to make contact.

If technology continues to evolve every minute for the better, why wouldn't you? When has technology been wrong? Think about that: when have we invented a new form of technology and then, a few months later, went backwards? It may not have been mastered yet, but it always sets the foundation for the next step.

Personal Notes & Ideas

build your network, grow your audience

Social media has taken us global. It has given YOU the easiest way to connect to a growing audience. Do you know how many people are born a day? About 400,000 new humans come in to this world daily. How many new users signed up to Facebook yesterday? A reported 600,000 plus has been an average daily amount for them. Networks like FB, Twitter, and Google have populations growing faster than the earth itself. These facts are what make social media a fact. It's not just in one country or area; the world has embraced it. Is it any wonder that every, let me say that again, EVERY major corporation has a Facebook, LinkedIn, and Twitter account now? Why? They know the power of it, and, more importantly, they know how to USE it.

In real estate, we "farm" a neighborhood or area of town. I don't know about you, but that's not good enough for me anymore. How about "farming earth"? Network around the world. Be a source in your profession who has the power to deal with or refer clients around the world to your associates. You can become the first call to anyone and build a team for that individual locally. Personally, I strongly feel you should be with a big-name company in real estate, one with a global brand. Why? Most large companies already have massive networks established that now allow a business associate to keep in touch with other associates around the world through social media. Add your own network to a large company's network, and the possibilities are limitless. I have learned this first-hand.

Example: In real estate, it is common to refer a deal to an agent in another area and ask for a 25% referral fee. Sometimes the agent will try to find an agent themselves or go through their relocation dept. to find them one in that out-of-area location. Regardless, if they find one or the re-lo dept. does, it still goes through the company and everyone gets paid. But what about when an agent is referring a deal to your area and has no idea who you are? They of course go through their company, and the deal is referred to whomever—chances are, not you. However, what if being with this large company has made it possible to meet agents from everywhere? Their network and your social media combined make it very easy to meet new agents on the social networks.

Well, now take that same scenario from above...you really think that agent you would have never known—but now that you're on each other's Facebook—is still going to call a random agent or re-lo first? Or are they going to call that one agent on their FB out in California who always has those great posts who they have been able to get to know? You get the referral, they get paid, and the company re-lo dept. gets paid. The only difference is they chose the agent this time, one that they knew. You see, you can create and build your own relocation network right at your fingertips, which only benefits you and the company.

This is another reason social media is growing non-stop. People are using it for what it is: networking and meeting people. Do you walk into a networking event or gathering and wait for people to come up to you and introduce themselves? No, we would never meet and connect that way; we are 'people-persons,' and if social media has become the new and unbelievable way to meet and connect, then do exactly that: go meet and connect!

I am not saying to not focus on your local area as a great agent. I am saying to use social networking for what it is: another source. Remember the saying "I'd rather have 1% of a hundred men's efforts than 100% of my own"? Well, how about in real estate? Wouldn't you rather have 25% of a hundred agents' efforts around the world in addition to 100% of your own local efforts? Uhh, yeah!

The power of brand and the power of numbers to me are necessities in business. Now I know you may work for a small company and may disagree with this. But it's a fact: you will get more business now more than ever before with a big name behind you simply because of social media and online presence playing such a huge part today. I do know agents who are with small agencies that are dominating in their business with social media. But I personally have seen what the difference is when integrating social media while working with a small firm, and then exploding when I moved to an international firm. One example that made me realize this was when I was referred a new athlete as a client out of state. I deal with athletes quite a bit and this was a first. At the time I was with a small company and I needed to refer the deal out of state. I value staying involved with even my referred transactions. My clients feel at that point that I didn't just refer them off to anyone. However, with a small company that had no presence in this particular state, I referred my client to a different company. I immediately got a call from my client asking me why they were now working with a different company. "Are you not in this state?" they asked. To make a long story short, I was able to stay involved and keep the deal together but that is when I realized never again.

My client even advised me that with the other athletes they would be referring me, I might seriously want to move to a national brand. After a couple referrals where I was simply referring the athletes within my same company, there was never a question or concern on their part. Especially since, most of the time, I am referring them to a top agent for that area. I also enjoy referring them in person by traveling there myself for the initial meet and greet.

Bottom line, these companies were already big before, and now since they have embraced social media correctly, they are only getting bigger and more dominant. You may also say it's because they don't initially give you as high of a commission split as the small companies do, but it's what else they give you that far outweighs this. Training, networking, marketing, and power beyond what words can explain. You have to see it to believe it. They didn't get this large for no reason; they got this large because thousands of agents over time saw the same benefits and helped that company rise to that level. This is usually the case in most professions of individual sales associates. In real estate you have companies like Coldwell Banker, Keller-Williams, Remax, Sothebys, C-21, Prudential, etc. Insurance companies like, Allstate, Farmers, State-Farm, Liberty Mutual, Progressive, etc. Bottom-line, your social network combined with the large network of the company you work for is unbeatable.

If you're meeting people and going to be networking with social media, don't you think it's important for them to identify something about you they already know? "Oh, this person has a few mutual friends and also works for that large, well known company I see signs and ads for." This may be hard to grasp, but I am living proof that this type of understanding of social media works. You simply need to treat connecting with people within social media as if you were sitting with the person over coffee, meeting them for the first time. What is the most important aspect of meeting someone new? Something to talk about, right?

Networks like Facebook, Google+, and LinkedIn are a world within, as I have shared, not a profile page. You know by now that social media is no longer a MySpace account for a college student. Everything these large social networks as a whole are accomplishing is due to the fact they are evolving as quickly as they were created.

Take Facebook: it is becoming a one-stop shop. You can use it as a search engine, email, website, networking, advertising, selling, buying...it goes on forever. In all honesty, Facebook is its own Internet service. Its own spider 'web,' per se.

Remember how I said social media is growing at a faster rate than earth itself? Facebook alone, with its average 600k to 700k new sign-ups a day, has hit the 700 million users mark, which is estimated to hit 1 billion in 2012! One billion? This is the new Internet, the new 'web.'

Personal Notes & Ideas

CHAPTER 7

too good to be true?

Not only is social media NOT too good to be true, but it's free for the most part. Remember the old saying "nothing in life is free"? I have tried to look for this to be the case with social media, but simply can't see it. It is free and it works. Even crazier is how every day more and more people are making these social networks like the 'FAB 5' their main websites. Many business owners I have trained do not have a traditional website anymore. The 'FAB 5' together are billion-dollar empires with a billion users that enable us to access and network within their networks at no cost.

In a time of economic crisis and income being less than it once was, social media not only is the better way to market, advertise, and network, but, being free, it has made it so we don't have to spend the money we once did on print ads all over the place. We can now use that money toward video marketing and possibly placing ads on the social networks. These ads are a thousand times more effective, too—proven!

With how everything is searched, tracked, and found today, online presence is everything. Personally I feel social media and these networks are single-handedly saving the rain forest. Ok, maybe we can't go that far yet, but think about what it's replacing. Paper, paper, and more paper. ☺

For the first time in history, we no longer have to worry about our ad campaigns being sharp enough for a consumer to call us on.

With the web and social media, they immediately can see us, learn about us, watch a video on us...you control what they know, but, better yet, you're finding them now, not waiting by the phone for it to ring. You're making buyers out of people who didn't realize they were buyers, investors of people who didn't realize they were investors, customers who didn't realize they were customers, etc. You see, we no longer search for information; information searches for us.

In 2010, one of the first times I saw how the game was changing so quickly was with one of the homes I sold. I listed a multi-million-dollar property and started a massive online campaign with it on all my networks, websites, partner sites, blogs, etc. Within 60 days, I got a call from someone outside the U.S. who wasn't even looking to buy a home. But the listing came across their screen through some site they were on, and the individual fell in love with it and just had to have it. It was found out later that someone had seen a post of a post about it, shared the post, and sent the link to the buyer. When everything was said and done, the home sold within six months, and I had gained a great client and had a new network of executives I was introduced to.

Ask yourself why all magazine companies now offer online presence on their websites when you run an ad with them.

They know that is where they themselves are getting the most traffic for their magazine. So of course they want it to work for us as well and already know that's what we want to hear. They see first-hand that traffic on their sites is far greater than the print magazines' effectiveness in distribution. Some magazines have even partnered up with other large websites to help them attract advertisers to run an ad, and not only will it be on the magazine's site, but it will automatically run on any partner sites they have set up.

Here is a magazine in my field, for example:

Homes and Land is a massive nationwide magazine for real estate ads, homes for sale, finance companies, etc. They are the number-one luxury home website in the world with millions of monthly hits. As an agent, when you run an ad with the magazine, you are then given a personal website within homesandland.com. Now your listing is on their site as well, but what most agents I talk to do not realize is that, in addition to their homes and land website, the magazine is partnered with websites like the *New York Times, Wall Street Journal, Zillow*, etc., and your listing automatically feeds in to those websites' real estate search tabs. So if someone in Chicago is on the *Wall Street Journal* and wants to click the real estate tab and search for properties in Los Angeles, guess what listing they will see? Yours! This is what I am talking about, friends: the power of numbers and the power of your online presence. Without it, as a rookie, you will NOT last; more importantly, as a veteran, if you don't want to adapt because times are great now, there is no doubt it will end before you were ready to retire. Your call, but there are a couple billion people who agree with me simply by their actions with online presence and growth in their personal business.

Social media ads: not free, but AMAZING!

Ok, maybe you want to spend some money now. This example is for the real estate agents, but if you're in a different profession, I want you to think about your occupation as well. Wouldn't it be awesome to call the magazine or newsletter you have always run ads in and ask them the following: "Please go hand this month's issue of my ad to only men and women between the ages of 25 to 65, within a 50-mile radius, in these zip codes, who have interests in Home Depot, do-it-yourself, Pier 1 Imports, Restoration Hardware, Lowes Home Improvement, and having a green thumb...thanks!" Well, we know the magazine staff would look at you like you were crazy and respond by saying, "Yeah...no, but a lot of our readers have those interests, so I'm sure they will call about your ad."

Well, Facebook ads can do exactly this! I can narrow down the exact demographic of consumer for whom I want my ad to pop up on the right-hand column of their social network profile pages. I can pay per click, or give a budget cap that automatically stops the ad when my budget cap has been met. The options are limitless.

An important factor in online presence is linking it all together—traffic is key! One of my favorite social network brand names is LinkedIn because it truly is the best name that explains it all. The entire globe is linked in now, and in that sense the entire globe is united. Notice how most websites now have the link buttons to their Facebook, Twitter, YouTube accounts and so on? Here is an example of mine...yes, this is my website only to show you my link buttons, not to take your time to navigate through it, as I said before when we were first discussing QR codes.

Websites have free downloads to their smart phone applications as well. There is a great book titled *The Web Is Dead.* It's not saying the web itself is dead; it's saying that just as the Internet continues to evolve and technology is always trying to make information faster and easier to access, websites are now the slow, boring way to find info, and it's the mini versions of those sites, like applications as well as the sites' social network pages, that get the traffic.

THE NEW WAY TO WATCH TV p.136
THE COOLEST GADGET PROTOTYPES OF ALL TIME!
THE MOST TOXIC TOWN IN AMERICA p.162

WIRED

The Web is dead.

WHAT AND
HAPPENED WHY
BY CHRIS ANDERSON BY MICHAEL WOLFF

Websites, although very important to have, have been replaced with personal and business social networks built by the professionals themselves, just like you. We live in a time when a professional's Facebook profile is without question a thousand times more effective than their website or lack of a website altogether, if that social network page is used correctly, of course. Using it to tag yourself in photos skydiving naked and/or taking body shots of rum may not work very well for your business. ☺ I know that's how social media started with MySpace and glamor pics, but it has now evolved into what it's going to stay at, which is the Internet itself: the social Internet.

Take, for instance, Facebook.com/Marketplace vs. Craigslist.

This is a perfect example of what social media is becoming...the marketplace on FB sells everything. Social network sites are taking over the Internet. Facebook is neck-in-neck with Google for the most logins a day; however, Google has been around much longer and is the number-one search engine. Now we have Google+, which is the new social aspect of Google, and I'm sure it will rise as a fantastic network from what I can see.

We are at the point where I can log in to Facebook or Google tomorrow morning and get whatever I need all day from their site. I can search stocks, email individuals, communicate with family, watch videos, buy a car, list one of my properties for sale on the marketplace, meet potential clients, search real estate values, never once leaving the site to another search engine—and that's just today. It's still advancing further every day. Why do you think Facebook rolled out the new email system so you have an actual Facebook email address? I'm TonyGiordano. info@Facebook.com.

I know: a bit long and complicated, but since FB rolled it out long after we all signed up for FB, we automatically get the address by whatever our user name URL was, which for me was www.Facebook.com/TonyGiordano.info. So if you are reading this book and are the individual who has Tony@Facebook. com, please call me—I want it! Lol!

In conclusion, you can see what has happened to the Internet recently with the birth of social media. It has taken over how we use the web. Here is a glimpse of that use...

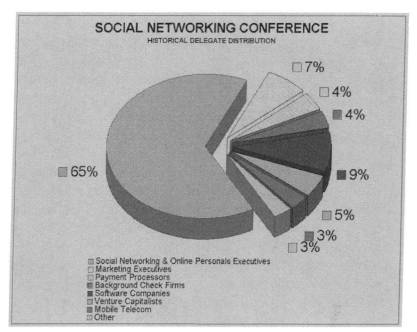

SOCIAL NETWORKING CONFERENCE
HISTORICAL DELEGATE DISTRIBUTION

□ 7%

□ 4%

■ 4%

■ 65%

■ 9%

□ 5%

■ 3%

□ 3%

■ Social Networking & Online Personals Executives
□ Marketing Executives
□ Payment Processors
■ Background Check Firms
■ Software Companies
□ Venture Capitalists
■ Mobile Telecom
□ Other

Google Images 2011

Looking at this chart should make you realize what is happening. Remember the previous pie chart that showed the dominance of the Internet in effective marketing? Well, this pie shows what is dominant on the Internet. Why would you not want to focus on and integrate social media every day in your business? This is where everyone is. Obviously not everyone, but a vast majority of the people you want as clients are on social networks.

Example: I know the age group of, say, 60 and up may not be social networking very much compared to younger generations. We may still need to reach these clients by mail, telephone, etc. But whether it's real estate, cars, insurance, financial management, estate trusts, entertainment, etc., how many changes are happening this late in life? Not many. However, the age group of 20 to 50 makes up the majority of social networks, and how many changes are they making from the ages of 20 to 50? How many times are they going to change homes, cars, insurance, portfolios, careers, estates, etc.?

I was at a real estate summit recently and the speaker before me had told the audience that social media is important, but that mailers, cold-calling, door-knocking, and print ads are still effective in reaching people not on social networks. When it was my turn to speak, I simply agreed with that, but added, "Who are the people on Facebook, Twitter, Google+, etc.? They are an age group between 20 to 50 that will buy their first condo, then upgrade to a home, then get married and upgrade maybe one more time before settling. That was three transactions. The age group that may or may not be on these social networks is the older demographic that is retired and on average will be one transaction. What should your focus be for the longevity of your career?" Go where the people are; it is that simple, friends.

Personal Notes & Ideas

· ·
· ·
· ·
· ·
· ·
· ·
· ·
· ·
· ·
· ·
· ·
· ·
· ·
· ·
· ·
· ·

the feeling is "mutual"

Mutual: *Shared by more than one party or object*

with a common denominator

Ok, by now you have already added friends and family; now it's time to go meet people, interact, comment, etc. Do you recall when I said that the famous phrase "if you build it, they will come" does not work with social media? Remember, it's the way we communicate and express ourselves now, so go ahead and 'add as friend'!

Here is the KEY and one of my best-kept secrets…well, until this book is released, lol. Are you ready: "treat social media, social networks, like human beings"! Think about that for a second. By now we all realize social media is not what it started out as, rather that it's the new Internet. Then it's without question the newest and fastest-growing form of communication and staying tuned into world events. Then why shouldn't you treat it like a human?

Here is what I mean: now more than ever, someone will accept an 'add request' because you have mutual friends, faster than they would give you information on who they are in person. If you meet someone face-to-face and tell them you have a few mutual friends, do you think they will sit there and answer all your questions about where they grew up, likes and dislikes, religion, politics, maybe show you some photos on their phone of a recent vacation, all in the first few minutes of meeting you and trusting you? The answer is more than likely no. Yet they trust you on a social network with mutual friends, having never met you in their life. Well, that's because they know once they accept you as a new friend, they will learn a lot about you, too. It's not rocket science; it's called getting to know each other, and making friends, associates, and contacts—what we as people have always done...

Needless to say, we are 'people' people, and we of course all want to interact in person and shake someone's hand, and that's still very important, but I constantly meet people for the first time weeks after they have already been on a social network of mine and we are already good friends. It usually is a first-time greeting consisting with a warm embrace because we already have so much in common and feel we know each other so well because, in all honesty, don't we, for the most part? Whenever I am traveling somewhere to train a company or individual on this aspect of social networking, I will prove how this works in front of everyone and then the best sound comes next, when everyone gasps for air and the excitement starts. You while reading this book as well as before finishing this book, will see some of these examples.

I have often said humorously, *"I don't think we can say it's impolite to stare at people anymore; we are simply trying to figure out if we are on each other's Facebook!"*

Start meeting new people by getting involved, commenting, discussing, and giving compliments. Communication manners still exist in social media; you must have them and make them a habit. As you start to use the lessons and techniques of this book in your social networking, you will see the importance of treating it as a human. If you post, tweet, and/or share something on your wall, maybe something funny, and people are commenting on it, then make sure to 'like' their comment. Make sure to comment back and say thank you.

Take, for instance, if you were standing in front of them in person and they said to you, "That was a really great thing you did. I love hearing your stories..." Would you just stand there and stare at them and say nothing back? Of course not! You would say thank you and respond. Well, the same rules apply in this level of social media interaction. As you do this, you will start to see improvement in your business and online traffic.

Stalking? No, it's communicating. We all know and understand the difference, I hope! I hear the excuse so many times that someone is afraid they are going to seem like they are a stalker trying to meet someone new. First, you have mutual friends; second, relax—if they don't accept you, maybe they want to meet you first or ask one of your mutual friends about you. Stalking is when they ignore your request and you don't get the picture and keep requesting and need to be blocked entirely. Gotta love that feature! ☺ Now, I am not saying to just start adding random people by the dozens and dozens. Facebook will suspend you for a couple days on add requests if they feel you are just trying to ask any and all people. Add people who you have engaged with or met via another friend's post and comment log—people you have common interests with. Bottom line: have fun with it, friends. Personally, I love and enjoy meeting people in any way and any place—well, except in jail. That's probably not a good place...lol.

Friend suggestions are a great way to connect with new people. Feel free to ask a friend who you respect a lot and is a business professional to suggest you as a friend to all their friends. Some may ask you based on the suggestion to be their friend, but it's also a great way to follow up with a personal add request down the road. They will remember their friend's suggestion about you. How many times have we asked a friend or someone we know to introduce us to someone or refer us to someone? See how you treat it the same way? I will say, in the last couple years I have met many people who have become great friends and business contacts from social media by doing just this.

Tip—Send a message with your request; say "hi."

Sending a message is a nice gesture. Would you ever go up to someone on the street and, before introducing yourself, walk right up to them, stare them in the eyes, grab their hand, and shake it first? Probably not, and if you did, I'm sure you can imagine what their response might be, lol.

But, seriously, you request someone as a friend and say, "Hello, it seems we have some 'mutual friends' but we've never had the chance to meet in person. Why do you think Bob, Jane, and Nancy don't want us to meet? Lol! In any case, nice to meet you!" If they don't at least reply to you, probably not someone you would have done well with in person, either.

In addition to sending a note, always make sure to thank them for accepting your request...simply courteous. I try to always say "thanks for the add" on the walls of their profile.

Personal Notes & Ideas

. . . .
. . . .
. . . .
. . . .
. . . .
. . . .
. . . .
. . . .
. . . .
. . . .
. . . .
. . . .
. . . .
. . . .
. . . .
. . . .
. . . .
. . . .

create content, create contacts

Create: *Cause (something) to happen as a result of one's actions*

I can't express it enough, but *if you 'just' build it, they 'won't' come.*

Start with creating content that your friends and family know you for. Example: if your friends and family know you to be funny, then be funny, but give it a business twist. I love being motivational every day. I will post either my own quotes or great quotes from history. I always link my website with the quote, which creates traffic to it. People will read the post, like or comment on it, and while they are at it, click your link and maybe surf around on your website for a bit. I know this works because times I post, share, and link my website, I see the increase of hits to my website on that day. You see, it's also staying in tune with your analytics. Your website stats. That is how you see it work first-hand.

You need to be a reason to add, follow, like, watch, subscribe to... No one knows who you are really and no one really cares about your open house this weekend, from what I have learned.

We especially all should know that no one cares if we are eating a Big Mac at the intersection of 5th and Main St. ☺

It's the way you post and share that counts. I will be out and about and countless times will meet someone in person who is already on my Facebook or some other social network of mine, and they tell me, "Tony, I really enjoy your posts. When I first got your friend request, I was wondering who this guy was with mutual friends. Looked on your wall and read some of your posts and thought you were an interesting person to stay in touch with." It gives me such a great feeling when I hear that. I am really just doing what I would like everyone to do: be happy in life and stay in touch.

The business will come simply because they enjoy their new relationship with you, and when they think real estate (or whatever profession you are in), they will think of you. This example is why I personally keep my posts at a public setting for 'Everyone' to see, so that when they see my request, they can do a little research first on who I am, and see my posts and basic info. This gives them a reason now to accept or follow me back because they found it interesting.

Let's talk a little "business" page now. I do have a business page people can 'like' and it's set up for the most part, but I'm still meeting new people on my personal profile. I'm still getting friend requests from other people. So my opinion, and it seems to work for not only me but everyone I teach in sales, is that I want to be my clients' friend, too. I want people to get to know me as I am getting to know them. Not just 'like' my business page, because who am I, right? Unless you're going to be on TV anytime soon, no one knows who you are. Celebrities, politicians, athletes get thousands and even millions of people to 'like' and 'follow' them because we know who they are. That's why we have to go meet people ourselves. You have to show them your content is worth following. I'm sure one day I will exercise the option Facebook has now to convert the personal page and all my friends over to the business page, but, for now, I'm still building, I'm still networking, and I'm enjoying every minute of it.

I heard a Google executive once say the most important aspect to social media was 'The Four E's,' as he called them.

ENGAGE, EXCITE, EDUCATE, EVANGELIZE

First, **ENGAGE** your friends and contacts. This means to interact and do what I have been saying to do: have a conversation. That's what social media is and that's how it works. If you don't converse, you are forgotten by the people who don't know you well on the social network. Your family and friends still see and hear from you, but the online friends and contacts do not. A common mistake I see is agents or business professionals only posting business, listings, and work-related content. This is not effective. *It is called social media, not work media, so be social* and reap the rewards!

Second, **EXCITE** your friends and contacts. In my opinion, this happens by saying thank you when they comment on your posts. EXCITE happens when you say "happy birthday" to someone when your profile reminds you whose BDs are that day. We all love attention; we all get excited when we receive it. Comment on friends' posts and interact with other people commenting on their posts. This is a great way to meet and add new friends. 'Like' someone's comment and then follow it up with an add request. Another way is to simply be exciting, motivating, inspirational—isn't that what we all want?

Third, **EDUCATE** your friends and contacts. They like you by now, they respect you, they know about your likes, interests, family...so now give them a little education about what you do in subtle ways. But don't go overboard and stick your business down their throats. Realtors and business professionals are community people, social people, so give your postings social content with a business twist. Discuss your community, interests, etc. The key is staying in their mind when it comes to your profession not because you talk about business all the time. For my industry readers, here is an example.

<u>Non-subtle post:</u> 'Come by and visit me this weekend at my open house on Ocean Ave. If you can't, let me know if you know anyone wanting to buy a home.' (In my opinion, not only are you telling them what to do, but you are also coming across like you're begging a bit.) Yes, any content is good per se, but I have learned that certain content can be a thousand times more effective. Take, for instance...

<u>Subtle post:</u> 'Congratulations to my clients on the purchase of their first home. This is why I love my job: very rewarding! <u>www.TonyGiordano.net</u>'

Another subtle way of reminding people what you do is 'Checking In' to your office location on Facebook. People use check-ins all the time with services like Four Square.

EXAMPLE: Tory DuVarney is at **Handsome Devil Clothing Headquarters (Ventura Beach Ca. 93001)**.

You can also educate by sharing an article, or maybe stating a fact about your industry that is sometimes forgotten.

Fourth, ***EVANGELIZE.*** Not in the religious aspect is this word being used, but in the same sense that now you have made believers in you who would have never known who you were. At this point they are more than likely preaching to others about you. Suggesting you and referring people and business to you. They are friends now; maybe you have met some in person at this point. They also know and see that you have clients that trust you. They have learned from you, maybe they are inspired by you, but, most importantly, they know you feel the same about them. This isn't artificial; it's using the amazing tool of social media to meet people, to network, to learn, and to communicate.

RSS feeds are a great way in helping you create content. RSS feeds are where you have articles and content that downloads (feeds) automatically on to your walls and websites from another website. For me, any article my company posts about our industry, I have RSS feed on to my business page. If you do this, make sure it's a site where you don't mind all of their content feeding into your site. Otherwise, if it's a news site and they post about your industry having problems or something negative, then that just posted to your wall and told all your contacts. So if you're with a big company that has national and international news, it's usually okay to RSS their info, because you know that anything they are willing to post, you should, too. This is another reason, in my opinion, why there is such an advantage in choosing a large company brand to work for.

I also have custom Home Search buttons (tabs) on my business page of FB, and you can create really any type of personal button for yourself and your profession, stock quotes, politics, music, art, entertainment, etc. As always, you can easily YouTube search a 'how to do' video on creating a custom button or buttons for your pages or how to set up the RSS feed, etc.

Don't be negative or share controversial opinions if you are going to be focusing on business. Yes, I know about freedom of speech, but we are not talking about self-expression in this book; we are talking about how to correctly engage social media to increase business growth. There are certain things we don't discuss with business associates or clients. Remember, if you want to express yourself, we already went over how to do that with your groups you have created and only allowing certain people to see and view it. Remember, the same manners in person are the same manners with social media and I don't think many of us would get into a debate with a new potential client. I know sometimes we may be negative or opinionated, but usually we only are if it's for a good cause or trying to make something negative into something positive.

Tip—A great way to interact is to ask questions

We as business professionals have to keep opinions to ourselves sometimes, but we are humans, and we all think our opinion is right. So in that case, allow other people to have opinions.

Ask a question and enjoy people's comments. They will love it because it's an opportunity to express themselves. I will constantly ask a question or for some advice and am shocked how many share their points. Whether I'm asking where is a good restaurant to eat at, a good dentist, how do you think the president did on his speech last night, etc., these are all great ways to keep your traffic and content up and stay in their minds. It is the power and effectiveness of social interaction, whether in person or online.

Personal Notes & Ideas

social media: fad or fact?

Fad: *A fashion, manner of conduct, that is taken up with great enthusiasm for a brief period of time; a craze*

Well, here we are: the last chapter. More of an overview of what you read. Is it as complicated as you may have thought? What have you learned? How do you feel about social media now? Do you believe it is how the world communicates and expresses itself now? How they network, connect, and market? I think it's safe to say we are not talking about bell bottoms here, friends. This is a global revolution that is proving itself daily. Anything that has gone global like social media, and I mean truly global, is not a fad. It is most of the time a necessity in communication at some level. Think about fact of necessity for these global 'fads' or 'facts.'

Cars: Fad or Fact?
Planes: Fad or Fact?
Radio: Fad or Fact?
Mail: Fad or Fact?

TV: Fad or Fact?
Internet: Fad or Fact?
Social Media: Fad or Fact?

Social networks are now the first form of communication
and expression in natural disasters. Social media has made it
easier for government and aid resources to pinpoint exact locations of natural disasters and where the aid is needed most simply based on people's 'tweets.' Twitter has proven time and time
again that social media is the new breaking news we tune in to,
whether it has been used by a country to tell the world about
current riots before they get too out of hand, or lives rescued
in the masses before possibly being lost. Just so you get what I
am saying, if you don't have a Twitter account, realize by the time
you hear breaking news on the TV or radio, millions have already
been tweeting about it for a while on Twitter. I have posted and
said before, "We no longer have to be lured in to staying on a TV
channel to hear about a story at the 'top of the hour' or 'news at
11.' Now, as soon as they say what's coming up later, I just search
it on Twitter, hear and read the entire story, and then go on with
my night while millions wait for the 'news at 11.'"

It has even gotten to the point where politicians announce
running for office on Twitter before a press release. Think about
that for a second. We all not only witnessed Facebook helping
President Obama in his campaign, but saw he was the first president who was not willing to get rid of his smart phone.

The other day I was watching one of the preliminary presi-
dential debates and the interviewer looked at the camera and
said, "If you have a question at home you would like answered,
please Facebook or Twitter us at..." Serious? Yes, serious!

Embrace it, friends—use it for what it is. After you've read
this book, I shouldn't have to say what that is anymore, right!?
Con...nec...ti... ☺

I will say that about 80% of my business in real estate comes
from Facebook alone. Let me break down a couple examples.

Remember in Chapter 7, the example I gave you about the listing back in 2010 that I sold in 6 months? That client actually came to me via a friend on Facebook. This individual knew dozens of well-qualified agents but chose me. Why? I stayed in his mind, like we have spoken about, from postings, comments, talking about the networks I am involved with that help my clients sell their homes, the teams of agents I build and co-list with to move property more quickly, and so on. Social media expression allowed me to stay in their mind in subtle ways so the day they heard real estate, they thought of me first. So that is deal one in this example.

Now, once the house sold, I posted a congratulations to my client on the sale, which was a spec home. Someone on my Facebook, whom I have never met in person, saw this post, "Congratulations to my client on the sale of his 5.250M spec property. Sold in six months! So happy for you..." The individual emailed me on FB and asked me if I ever list property outside the U.S. or help market property. I said being with a large company makes it very easy to contact my associates across the world to handle any property. They referred me a family member of theirs who was trying to sell their estate in another country. I contacted one of my associates in that area and set up a meeting at the estate. Between the power of them locally and the power of me blogging, online marketing, and social networking the property, we got the listing. So didn't deal two come from FB as well?

Now, after some time starting to post about the listing, blogging, etc., the agent I referred that deal to asked me if I would help market other listings they have through my social networks and channels. We came to an agreement and here comes deal three, four, and five. So even though they came from the agent, where did the agent come from? FB and the other client, FB and deal one that started it all, via FB. That is why I know 80% of my business comes to me via social networking. This is on a local and international level that door-knocking and open houses could never compete against.

Time and time again, a call or email comes to me immediately after a post of mine where someone has some questions they would like to ask me about buying or selling a property. It is this easy, friends. Of course we have to know what we are doing once we get the listing or business, which I am sure we all do, but it's how we can generate the business now like never before.

We know social media has had a MASSIVE impact on EVERYTHING! It really has changed the game in every way. It teaches, it learns, it evolves, it buys, it sells, it's global.

There is no question we live in a faster, abbreviated society: OMG, LOL, TTYL, THX, BFF, BTW, TMI, FYI, LMAO, LYSM, and so on and so on. I guess XOXO started it all. We are a 'mobile' society that finds someone who is not 'mobile' complicated and an inconvenience when trying to reach them via call, email, text, etc. Websites are now smart-phone applications that allow us to navigate more easily and freely from our mobile devices.

We are seeing the beginning of the QR code explosion that is making information easier to receive. In the real estate industry, they are on our ads, 'for sale' signs, websites, and social networks. They are an easy and fast way for someone to get all the info on the property for sale and not need to worry about the flyer box being empty. I have seen them used as insurance quotes, stock quotes, legal codes for attorneys, 'how to' directions, medical info, and many more. In fact business cards today are adding the QR code and only having your name and QR code on them because someone can just scan it and save your info into their phones. Save some trees while we are at it... ☺

Yes, not everyone has the ability to own a smart phone and hold it up to a QR code to open info, pictures, or a website, but there is no question they will. How do I know that? Because I haven't seen someone using a 'brick' phone recently—remember those? But I do see any and all people with cell phones today that once were the best phones on the market and now are basic. Eventually, smart-phone technology today will be in every hand and newer smart-phone technology will be even more advanced.

If you take anything from this book, I hope it's the importance of adaptability and how easy social networking can be. As I said before, it is not rocket science. You will without question see the rewards and gain business from social media if you apply this book and use these networks in the way I have. There are thousands of people out there who train individuals on this, but I wanted to pass on to my colleagues what I have learned and where I see that it works best, with actual experiences and examples of mine. It is easy for someone to say "go do it," but it is a thousand times more productive when they show you how they did it and are still doing it today. I hope I was able to do that for you and would love to hear from you soon on how it has worked for your business.

In the end, if social media did not account for millions more in volume in my business in just the last two years alone, then I could not have written this book. It is living proof that it works if you adapt and take these lessons and strategies and execute them in your career. We have been given the ability to network in ways never dreamed of—and anywhere in the world. I wish you the best success. One thing I firmly believe in and say every day on Facebook is:

THINK IT | ACT IT | SUCCEED IT

Made in the USA
San Bernardino, CA
03 July 2016